JOKES,
RIDDLES,
FUNNY STORIES

JOKES,

RIDDLES, FUNNY STORIES

Compiled by OSCAR WEIGLE
Illustrated by CROSBY NEWELL

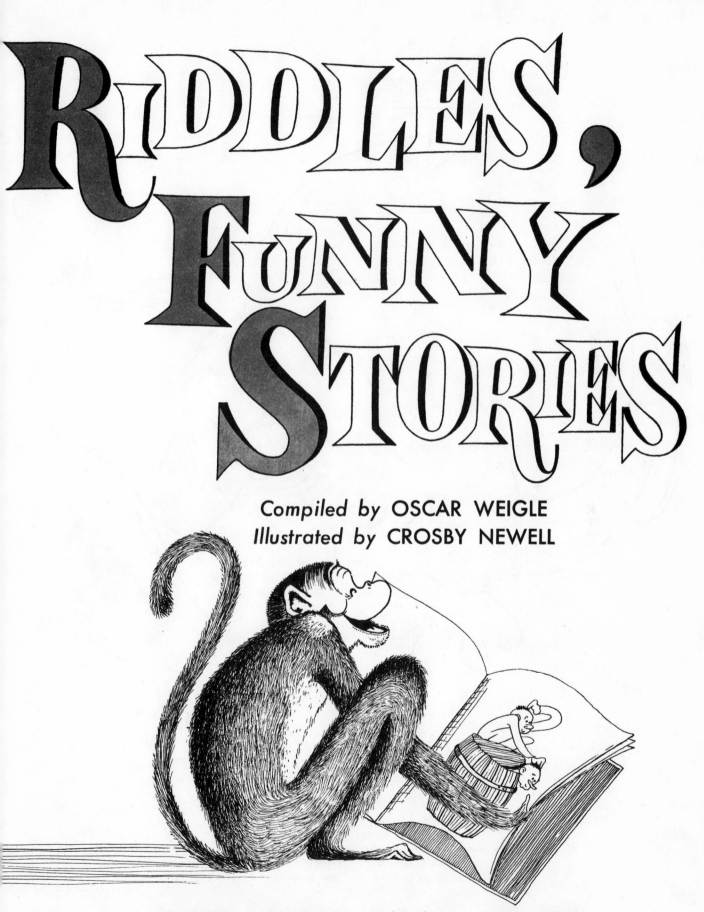

GROSSET & DUNLAP · Publishers · NEW YORK

1980 Printing
© 1959 by Grosset & Dunlap, Inc.
Published simultaneously in Canada.   Printed in the United States of America.
ISBN: 0-448-02892-1 (TRADE EDITION)   ISBN: 0-448-03210-4 (LIBRARY EDITION)

RIDDLE ME THIS

If one horse is shut up in a stable and another one is running loose down the road, which horse is singing, "Don't fence me in"?

Neither horse. Horses can't sing.

How do you make a slow horse fast?

Don't give him anything to eat for a while.

When is a shaggy dog most likely to enter a house?

When the door is open.

Why is a hill like a lazy dog?

Because a hill is an inclined plane. An inclined plane is a slope up. And a slope up (slow pup) is a lazy dog.

The clock strikes 13. What time is it?

Time to get the clock fixed.

Which has more legs — a horse or no horse?

No horse. No horse has eight legs, but a horse has just four legs.

What inventions have helped men up in the world?

The elevator, the escalator — and the alarm clock.

After the rain falls, when does it rise again?

In dew time.

What animal do you look like when you take a bath?

A little bear.

How do sailors get their clothes clean?

They throw them overboard and then they are washed ashore.

Why is a rabbit's nose always shiny?
Because he has the powder puff on the wrong end.

What's black and white and red all over?
An embarrassed zebra.

How do you spell mousetrap in three letters?
C-A-T.

What do you call a bull that's sleeping?
A bulldozer.

I never ask any questions, but I get many answers. What am I?
A doorbell.

Why do hens lay eggs only during the day?
Because at night they become roosters.

Why would a spider make a good outfielder?
Because it catches flies.

How can you make money fast?
Nail it to the floor.

What has two thumbs but no fingers?
A pair of mittens.

What flower tells what the teacher did when she sat on a tack?
Rose.

Why does a dog turn around several times before lying down?
Because one good turn deserves another.

What goes up to the door, but never comes in?
The sidewalk.

What is a zebra after it is five years old?
Six years old.

Why is paper money more valuable than coins?
When you put it in your pocket, you double it, and when you take it out, you find it still in creases.

Why don't women become bald as fast as men?
Because they wear their hair longer.

Why is a wig like a lie?
Because it's a false hood.

What nut is like a sneeze?
A cashew nut.

What country do you become on a cold morning?
Chile.

I'm once in every minute, twice in every moment, yet not once in a thousand years. What am I?
The letter M.

I'm lighter than a feather, yet harder to hold. What am I?
Your breath.

In what month do women talk the least?
February — because it is the shortest month.

What is the best thing to put into a pie?
Your teeth.

What kind of dress do you have, but never wear?
Your address.

What would a cannibal be who ate his mother's sister?
An aunt-eater!

When do boats become very affectionate?
When they hug the shore.

What is the greatest feat of strength?
Wheeling, West Virginia.

I have four legs, yet only one foot. What am I?
A bed.

I'm something that always goes around a button. What am I?
A goat. (A goat always goes around a-buttin'.)

If two is company and three is a crowd, what are four and five?
Nine.

Why is a bride unlucky on her wedding day?
Because she doesn't marry the best man.

What is the best way to find someone out?
Go to his home when he isn't in.

If a carrot and a cabbage race, which will win?
The cabbage — because it's a head.

What did the rug say to the floor?
"Don't move! I've got you covered."

Why is a pencil like a riddle?
Because it's no good without a point.

Why is it useless to send letters and telegrams to Washington?
Because he is dead.

When should a baker stop making doughnuts?
When he gets tired of the hole business.

Why is an island like the letter T?
Because it's in the middle of water.

If Washington's wife went to Washington while Washington's washwoman washed Washington's woollies, how many W's in all?
There are no W's in "all"!

Why are tall people the laziest?
Because they are longer in bed than short people.

What speaks every word in the world?
An echo.

What's the best thing to put in an ice cream soda?
A straw.

If candy bars are ten cents in Boston, what are window panes in Philadelphia?
Glass.

What is worse than finding a worm in an apple?
Finding half a worm.

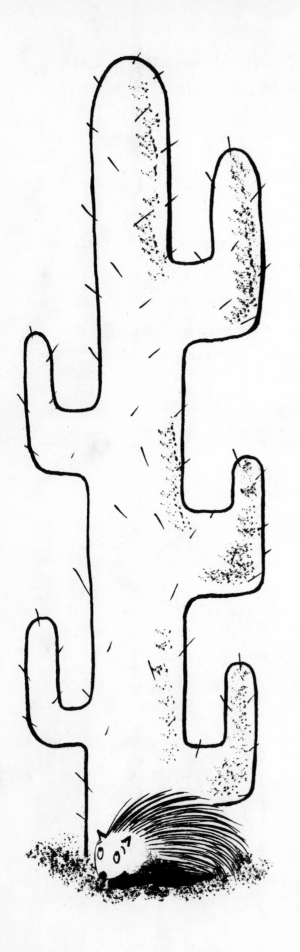

What did the porcupine say to the cactus plant?
"Is that you, Mama?"

What's the difference between a sewing machine and a kiss?
One sews seams nice, and the other seems so nice.

Which month has 28 days in it?
They all have.

What runs around a pasture but never moves?
A fence.

What's the difference between a motorman and a bad cold?
One knows the stops and the other stops the nose.

What do you sit on, sleep on, and brush your teeth with?
A chair, bed and toothbrush!

What did the South Pole explorer say to the North Pole explorer?
"Hello, you all!"

What kind of cloth would you buy to make a dress for a fat lady?
Broadcloth.

What grows down while growing up?
A duck.

What runs all around the yard, yet never moves?
The fence.

Why is it cheap to feed a giraffe?
Because he makes a little food go a long way.

Why was the Medieval Era called the Dark Ages?
Because it was knight-time.

What do you break by naming it?
Silence.

If you threw a black stone into the Red Sea, what would it become?
Wet!

What was the greatest bet ever made?
The alpha-bet.

What did the big toe say to the little toe?
"Don't look now, but there's a heel following us."

What did Paul Revere say at the end of his famous ride?
"Whoa!"

What is full of holes, and yet holds water?
A sponge.

Mr. Green is a butcher. He is six feet tall and wears a size ten shoe. What does he weigh?
Meat.

What goes 99-clump! 99-clump! 99-clump!?
A centipede with a wooden leg.

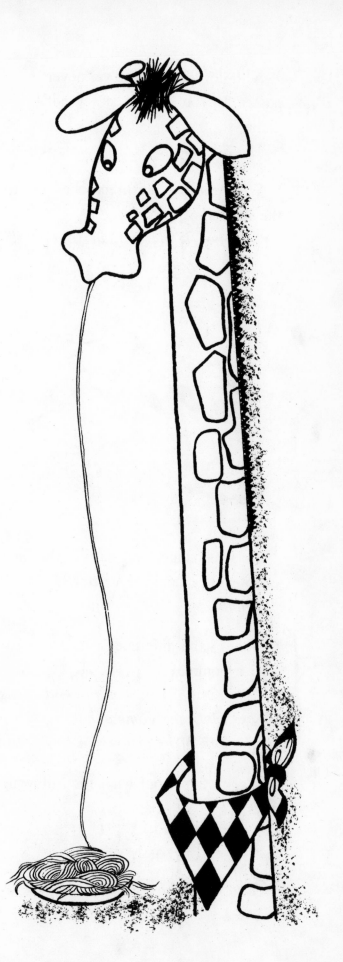

A tailor whom you've never seen passes by on the street. What's his name?

Mr. So-and-so. (Mr. Sew-and-sew)

What did the big firecracker say to the little firecracker?

"My pop is bigger than your pop!"

In what language should the last chapter of a book be written?

Finnish.

What's the difference between a cat and a comma?

The cat has claws at the end of its paws, while the comma has its pause at the end of its clause.

Try to figure out what the following says:

YY U R YY U B
I C U R YY 4 ME

Too wise you are, too wise you be,
I see you are too wise for me.

If a biscuit is a soda cracker, what is an ice pick?

A water cracker.

Why was the little strawberry worried?

Because his mother and father were in a jam.

Why is a heart like a policeman?

It has a regular beat.

What letter isn't found in the alphabet?

The one you mail.

What starts with a T, ends with a T, and is full of T?

A teapot.

I can run, but can't walk. What am I?

A stream.

I have teeth, but can't eat. What am I?

A comb.

What is it that will go up a chimney down, but won't go down the chimney up?

An umbrella.

Which side is the left side of a pie?

The side that isn't eaten.

What's the difference between an old penny and a new dime?

Nine cents.

What state doesn't feel so good?
Ill.

What state is a doctor?
Md.

What state is a father?
Pa.

What state is a number?
Tenn.

What state was important to Noah?
Ark.

What state is an unmarried woman?
Miss.

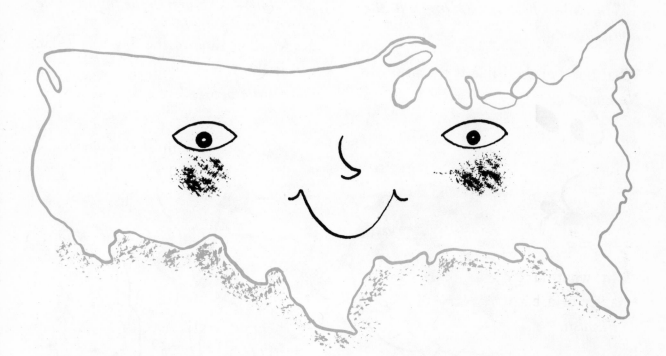

When is coffee like the soil?
When it is ground.

What part of a fish weighs the most?
The scales.

Why do white sheep eat more than black ones?
There are more of them.

When is a doctor annoyed the most?
When he is out of patients.

What is the best way to keep fish from smelling?
Cut off their noses.

If you were going through the woods, would you rather have a lion eat you or a bear?
The lion eat a bear!

What has the head of a cat, the tail of a cat, and yet isn't a cat?
A kitten.

BIBLICAL RIDDLES

Who was the straightest man in the Bible?

Joseph — because Pharaoh made a ruler out of him.

Who was the greatest actor in the Bible?

Samson — because he brought the house down.

What book of the Bible is a census?
Numbers.

What man in the Bible was the busiest doctor?

Job — he had more patience than anybody.

Who in the Bible was the champion runner of all time?

Adam — the first in the human race.

At what time of the day was Adam created?

A little before Eve.

'PUN MY WORD!

Say, did you read in the newspaper about the fellow who ate six dozen
    pancakes at one sitting?
No, how waffle!

Do you like your job, cleaning chimneys?
Soots me!

If you were locked in a room with nothing but a calendar and a bed, what
    would you eat and drink?
Eat the dates on the calendar and drink from the springs on the bed!

How much of that Swiss cheese did you eat?
The whole of it.

A Russian named Rudolph looked out of the window one morning and
    announced, "It's raining."
His wife looked out also and then said, "No, it's sleeting."
"It's raining," insisted the husband. "Rudolph the Red knows rain, dear!"

Reverend Martin and Reverend Gardner had a long telephone conversation this morning.
Hmm-m-m. Parson to parson, no doubt!

Why are telephone rates quite high in Iran?
Because everyone there speaks Persian to Persian.

I work in a candle company as a trimmer on Saturdays and Sundays.
Don't you work there the rest of the week?
No — just on wick ends.

Was your sister angry when she tried to get away from the skunk?
Not angry — but terribly incensed.

That suit fits you like a bandage.
Yes, I bought it by accident.

I think the library is on fire.
How can you tell it's the library?
I see volumes of smoke.

This suit is getting frayed.
'Fraid of what?

Where's the English channel?
It's not on *my* TV set!

There's the Dog Star.
Are you Sirius?

What did the beaver say to the tree?
It's been nice gnawing you.

Have you read "Freckles"?
No, just plain old brown ones.

I understand that your wife likes to talk.
Yes, she's been that way ever since she went home to mutter.

Do you think that if I wash, my face will be clean?
Let's soap for the best.

Why are you always so friendly with waitresses?
I play for large steaks.

Why does that letter bring tears to your eyes?
It's written on onion skin.

How did you know you needed a shave?
A little beard told me!

Baby candle: Mama, I feel hot.
Mama candle: Hush, dear, it's only glowing pains.

What is your gross income?
I have no gross income.
But how can that be?
I have a net income. I'm a fisherman.

What are taxes?
Little nails.

Why don't you shoo the flies?
Aaa-a, let 'em go barefoot!

What did the pencil say to the paper?
I dot my eyes on you!

Did you hear about the worm who joined the Army?
No.
He's in the apple corps.

Don't you know that everybody loves a fat man?
Yes, but they make up jokes at his expanse.

Is this a real Hawaiian band?
No, but everyone thinks it is because it plays everything in wacky-key.

TONGUE TWISTERS

A skunk sat on a stump.
The stump thunk the skunk stunk.
The skunk thunk the stump stunk.

Cross crossings cautiously.

Six snakes, slipping and sliding.

Bisquick — kiss quick.

Tim, the thin twin tinsmith.

Strange strategic statistics.

She sells sea shells by the seashore.

The sun shines on the shop signs.

She stood at the door of Mrs. Smith's fish-sauce shop, welcoming him in.

Peter Piper picked a peck of pickled peppers.
Did Peter Piper pick a peck of pickled peppers?
If Peter Piper picked a peck of pickled peppers, where's the peck of
    pickled peppers Peter Piper picked?

Theophilus Thistle, the successful thistle-sifter,
While sifting a sieve full of unsifted thistles,
Thrust three thousand thistles through the thick of his thumb.
Now, if Theophilus Thistle, while sifting a sieve full of unsifted thistles,
Thrust three thousand thistles through the thick of his thumb,
See that thou, while sifting a sieve full of unsifted thistles,
Thrust not three thousand thistles through the thick of thy thumb!
(Success to the successful thistle-sifter!)

THE BUTTER BETTY BOUGHT

Betty Botta bought some butter.
"But," said she, "this butter's bitter!
If I put it in my batter,
It will make my batter bitter.
But a bit o' better butter
Will but make my batter better."
So she bought a bit o' butter
Better than the bitter butter,
Made her bitter batter better.
So 'twas better Betty Botta
Bought a bit o' better butter.

Sheep shouldn't sleep in a shack.
Sheep should sleep in a shed.

If a Hottentot tot taught a Hottentot tot to talk e'er the tot could totter, ought the Hottentot tot be taught to say aught, or naught, or what ought to be taught her?

If to hoot and to toot a Hottentot tot be taught by a Hottentot tutor, should the tutor get hot if the Hottentot tot hoot and toot at the Hottentot tutor?

The crow flew over the river with a lump of raw liver in his mouth.

She sawed six slick, sleek, slim, slender saplings.

There's blood on the rubber baby buggy bumpers.

HOW'S BUSINESS?

Tailor: "Just sew-sew."

Electrician: "It's pretty light."

Farmer: "Mine is growing."

Refrigerator Salesman: "Not so hot."

Garbage Collector: "It's picking up."

Astronomer: "It's looking up."

Elevator Operator: "It has its ups and downs."

Optician: "It's looking better."

Author: "Mine is all write."

FARM FUNNIES

That new man I hired yesterday doesn't know much about farmin'.

How's that?

He found some milk bottles behind the barn and then came up to me and
said he'd found a cow's nest.

Visitor: What do you do with all the fruit that grows around here?

Farmer: Well, we eat what we can — and what we can't, we can!

Farmer: Down on the farm we go to bed with the chickens.
City Feller: Well, in town we'd rather sleep in our own beds.

Sy: What was your peach crop like this year?
Hy: Oh, a big storm blew down half of it — and we'd hardly gathered
    that when another big wind blew down the rest.
Sy: That's too bad. Could you do anything with the fruit you did pick up?
Hy: Yep. My wife ate one and I ate the other.

That horse you sold me is a fine animal, but I can't get him to hold
    his head up.
Well, that's because of his pride. He'll hold it up as soon as he's paid for.

Farmer: Where's that mule I told you to take out and have shod?
Hired Hand: Oh, did you say *shod?* I thought you said *shot!*

"We picked a few of your apples," the city motorists told the farmer as
    they drove away from his orchard. "We figured you wouldn't mind."
"Not at all," shouted the farmer after them. "While you were in the
    orchard I picked out some of your tools. I figured you wouldn't mind,
    either."

A farmer was trying desperately to get his mules to move forward, and
    getting close to losing his temper, when the local minister came by.
"You're just the man I want to see," said the farmer. "Tell me, Reverend,
    how did Noah ever get these critters into the ark?"

Just back from attending agricultural college, a young student paused to look over a farmer's orchard.

"You know," he said smugly, "your farming methods are really old-fashioned. Why, I'd be willing to bet you don't average ten pounds of apples from each of those trees."

"You'd be right," replied the farmer, snickering. "Them's pear trees!"

Why are you running that steam roller over your field?
Well, I figured I'd raise me some mashed potatoes this year.

A chicken farmer wrote to the Department of Agriculture as follows: "Gentlemen, something is wrong with my chickens. Every morning when I come out of the house I find two or three of them on the ground, cold and stiff, with their feet in the air. Can you please tell me what is the matter?"

In due time, back came a reply: "Dear sir, your chickens are dead."

Farmer: Can you tell me how long cows should be milked?
Prospective Handyman: They should be milked the same as short ones, of course.

"What's that over there?" a small boy wanted to know. He was from the city.
"That?" replied the farmer. "Why, that's a cow."
"And what are those things on its head?" the boy persisted.
"Those are horns," answered the farmer.
Just then the cow mooed.
"Which horn did it blow?" the boy wanted to know.

DAFFYNITIONS

Accordion: An instrument invented by the man who couldn't decide how big the fish was that got away.

Bacteria: The rear of a cafeteria.

Bamboo: An Italian baby.

Blunderbuss: Kissing the wrong girl.

Bread: Used in some restaurants to keep the insides of a sandwich from blowing away. It is also known as "raw toast."

Carbon: A famous opera.

Celery: Rhubarb with sound effects.

Children: Small people who are not permitted to act the way their parents did at that age.

Circle: A round straight line with a hole in the middle.

Cookbook: A stirring volume.

Dancing: The art of pulling your feet away faster than your partner can step on them.

Depth: Height turned upside down.

Divine: What grapes grow on.

Duck: A chicken in snowshoes.

Editor: A literary barber.

Egotist: A person of low taste, more interested in himself than in me.

Embarrassment: When you order something on the menu and find out that the orchestra is playing it.

Fission: A popular sport.

Grudge: A place to keep an automobile.

Home town: Where people wonder how you ever got as far as you did.

Hypochondriac: A person who just can't leave well enough alone.

Jury: Twelve men chosen to vote on which side has the better lawyer.

Nursery: Bawlroom.

Positive: Being mistaken at the top of one's voice.

Public speaking: Diluting a two-minute idea with a two-hour vocabulary.

Punctuality: The best way to avoid meeting people.

Reindeer: A horse with a TV antenna.

Rich man: One who doesn't know his son is in college.

Saddle: A city in Washington state.

Sandwich spread: What people get from eating between meals.

Screen door: Something the kids get a bang out of.

Secret: Something that's hushed about from place to place.

Senator: Half horse and half man.

Skeleton: Some bones with the people scraped off.

Snuff: Stuff that, if you don't feel well, you're not quite up to.

Statistician: A man who draws a mathematically precise line from an unwarranted assumption to a foregone conclusion.

Steam: Water crazy with the heat.

Sweater: A garment worn by a child when its mother feels chilly.

Woman: Someone who reaches for a chair when the telephone rings.

Zephyr: A breeze that got into a travel folder.

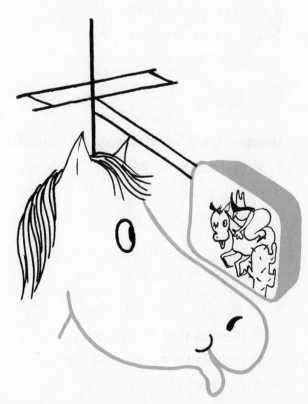

RHYMES WITH AND WITHOUT REASON

'Tis done beneath the mistletoe,
'Tis done beneath the rose,
But the proper place to kiss, you know,
Is just beneath the nose.

Jack be nimble,
Jack be quick,
Jack jump over the candlestick.
Big deal!

Hickory, dickory, dock,
Two mice ran up the clock,
The clock struck one,
But the other one got away.

OLD-FASHIONED FUN

By W. M. Thackeray

When that old joke was new,
It was not hard to joke,
And puns we now pooh-pooh,
Great laughter would provoke.

True wit was seldom heard,
And humor shown by few,
When reign'd King George the Third,
And that old joke was new.

It passed indeed for wit,
Did this achievement rare,
When down your friend would sit,
To steal away his chair.

You brought him to the floor,
You bruised him black and blue,
And this would cause a roar,
When your old joke was new.

If chlorophyll cures every ill,
It is my expectation
That it would pay to run some day
A chlorophylling station.

He rocked the boat,
Did Ezra Shank;
These bubbles mark
   O
   O
   O
   O
   O
Where Ezra sank.

He went out one lovely night
To call upon a miss,
And when he reached her residence,
                   this.
                like
            stairs
         up
      ran
He
Her father met him at the door,
He didn't see the miss.
He'll not go there again, though, for
He
  went
     down
        stairs
         like
           this.

I often pause and wonder
At fate's peculiar ways,
For nearly all our famous men
Were born on holidays.

Women's faults are many,
Men have only two:
Everything they say,
And everything they do.

At railroad crossings,
Here's how to figger:
In case of a tie,
The engine's bigger.

He ate a hot dog sandwich
And rolled his eyes above.
He ate half-a-dozen more,
And died of puppy love.

I eat my peas with honey,
I have done it all my life;
They do taste kind of funny,
But it keeps them on the knife.

"I guess it must be time to go,"
At last remarked the bore;
"A wonderful guess," she answered.
"Why didn't you guess before?"

"I love the ground you walk on."
This was the tale he told.
For they lived up by the Klondike
And the ground was full of gold!

Into the coop the rooster rolls an ostrich egg;
The hen he faces . . .
"Not to chide or deride, but only to show
What's being done in other places."

I never see my rector's eyes;
He hides their light divine —
For when he prays, he shuts his own,
And when he preaches, mine.

'Twixt optimist and pessimist,
The difference is droll:
The optimist sees the doughnut,
The pessimist sees the hole.

Don't worry if your job is small,
And your rewards are few;
Remember that the mighty oak
Was once a nut like you.

I sneezed a sneeze into the air,
It fell to earth I know not where;
Hard and cold were the looks of those
In whose vicinity I snooze.

LIMERICKS

There was a young fellow named Hall
Who fell in the spring in the fall.
    'Twould have been a sad thing
    If he'd died in the spring,
But he didn't — he died in the fall.

There was a young lady of Crete
Who was exceedingly neat.
    When she got out of bed,
    She stood on her head
To make sure of not soiling her feet.

There was an old person of Leeds,
And simple indeed were his needs.
    Said he, "To save toil,
    Growing things in the soil.
I"ll just eat the packets of seeds."

There was an old man of Peru
Who dreamed he was kissing his shoe.
    He awoke in the night
    In a terrible fright,
And found it was perfectly true!

There was a young man from Japan
Who wrote verse that never would scan.
    When they said, "But the thing
    Doesn't go with swing,"
He said, "Yes, but I always like to get
    as many words into the last line
    as I possibly can."

A very young girl — call her Emma —
Was seized with a terrible tremor.
 She had swallowed a spider
 Which stung her inside her —
Gadzooks, what an awful dilemma!

There was a young lady of Woosester
Who usest to crow like a roosester.
 She usest to climb
 Two trees at a time,
But her sisester usest to boosest her.

There was a young maid of Tralee
Whose knowledge of French was "Oui, oui."
 When they said, "Parlez vous?"
 She replied, "Same to you!"
She was famed for her bright repartee.

There was a young man from the West
Who with a young girl was obsessed.
 So hard did he press her
 To make her say, "Yes, sir!"
That he broke three cigars in his vest.

There was a young lady named Sue
Who saw a strange beast at the zoo.
 When she asked, "Is it old?"
 She was smilingly told,
"It's not an old beast, but a Gnu!"

There was a young man from the city
Who met what he thought was a kitty.
 He gave it a pat,
 And said, "Nice little cat."
And they buried his clothes out of pity.

There was a young man of Devizes
Whose ears were of different sizes.
 The one that was small
 Was of no use at all,
But the other won several prizes.

An epicure dining at Crewe
Found quite a large mouse in his stew.
 Said the waiter, "Don't shout,
 And wave it about,
Or the rest will be wanting one too."

THE KIDDY CORNER

Mother: Junior, there were two pieces of pie in the cupboard this morning and now there is only one. Can you explain that?
Junior: It was so dark I didn't see the other piece, Mommy.

Aunt Martha: And what are you going to give your baby brother for Christmas, Billy?
Billy: I don't know. I gave him the measles last Christmas.

Tommy, why did you put a frog in your little sister's bed?
Because I couldn't catch a mouse.

Mother: Eat your spinach, dear. It will put some color in your cheeks.
Little Boy: But Mom, I don't *want* green cheeks!

Little Andy was given an orange by a lady visitor. "What do you say to the nice lady?" his mother prompted him.
"Peel it," replied Andy.

Little Boy: I would like to buy a puppy. How much do they cost?
Pet Shop Owner: Ten dollars apiece.
Little Boy: Oh, but I want a whole one!

Well, Timmy, how do you like school?
Closed!

Teddy: Mommy, may I have a dime for the man who is crying outside?
Mother: Of course, dear. What is he crying about?
Teddy: "Ice cream — ten cents!"

Mother: Junior, what are you doing?
Junior: I'm feeding the monkeys half my peanuts.
Mother: That's nice.
Junior: Yes — I'm giving them the shells.

Little Richard, who enjoyed watching cowboy shows on TV, came home
from his first day at school and told his mother, "I've got to bring
a gun to school tomorrow."
"A gun!" exclaimed his startled mother. "Whatever do you need a gun
at school for?"
"The teacher," explained Richard, "told us that tomorrow we would all
learn how to draw."

Well, son, what did you learn in Sunday School today?
We learned all about a cross-eyed bear.
A *what?*
Yes, sir. We learned a song about him — "Gladly, the cross-eyed bear."

33

(Two-year-old youngster, reciting his sounds): "The dog says bow-wow. The cat says meow-meow. The duck says quack-quack. Mommy says no-no."

Father: Look at all of these bills! Rent, telephone, heating, clothes, food — the costs are going up on all of them! I'd be happy if just one thing went down!
Son: Daddy, here's my report card.

Father: How do you like your new teacher?
Danny: I don't like her at all.
Father: And why not?
Danny: She told me to sit up front for the present — and then she didn't give me the present.

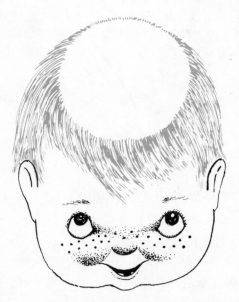

Barber: What kind of a haircut would you like, little boy?
Johnny: One like my father's — with a hole in the middle.

Father: Who was your mother talking to for an hour at the door?
Son: It was Mrs. Harris. She said she didn't have time to come in.

Father: This note from your teacher says that you missed every single question asked of you today. Do you have any explanation?
Son: Yes. None of the questions was in my category.

If I had 12 oranges and gave away 3, how many would I have left?

I don't know — in my class we do arithmetic with apples.

Junior: Mommy, do you remember that beautiful vase that's been handed down in our family for generations?

Mother: Yes, of course.

Junior: Well, this generation just broke it!

"Well, how did you like it?" the small boy's mother asked him as he walked into the house after his first day at school.

"I'm not going back tomorrow," he sighed.

"And why not?" his mother wanted to know.

"Oh," he replied, "it's just no use. I can't read, I can't write — and the teacher won't let me talk."

Mother: Now that you're a Boy Scout, Tommy, what will be your good deed for today?

Tommy: I'm going to teach that girl next door not to stick out her tongue at Boy Scouts!

Father: This report card says that you failed in everything but geography. Can you explain that?

Johnny: Sure. I don't take geography.

Timmy: Let's play school.

Jimmy: All right — but let's play I'm absent.

Mother: Eat your Jello, son.

Little Boy: It isn't dead yet.

May I have another cookie?

Another cookie, what?

Another cookie, please.

Please what?

Please, Mother.

Please, Mother, what?

Please, Mother, dear.

No, dear, you've had six already.

MEDICAL MIRTH

Doctor, every time I drink a cup of coffee I get a sharp pain in my eye. What should I do?

Just take the spoon out of your cup.

A man went to the doctor, his ear torn and bleeding. "I bit myself," he explained.

"That's impossible," the doctor said. "How can anyone bite himself in the ear?"

"I was standing on a chair," the man replied.

Patient: I'm having trouble with my breathing.
Doctor: I see. Well, I can give you something to stop that.

Joe: I suffered from insomnia for years before I went to see this doctor.
Moe: And what did he do for you?
Joe: He told my wife to stop playing the bagpipes in bed.

Doctor: How is your wife getting along on her reducing diet?
Husband: Wonderfully, Doctor. She vanished last night!

Doctor: What do you dream about at night?
Patient: Baseball.
Doctor: Don't you ever dream about anything else? Food, for instance?
Patient: What? And miss my turn at bat?

Patient: Remember when I came to you last year for my rheumatism? You
 told me to avoid dampness.
Doctor: Oh, yes, of course. And what can I do for you now?
Patient: I'd just like to know if it's all right to take a bath now.

Do you know what to do if a person faints?
Sure — turn him over so his face won't get dirty.

The psychologist was examining his patient.
"How many ears does a cat have?" he began.
"Two," the patient replied.
"And how many eyes does a cat have?"
"Two."
"And how many legs does a cat have?"
"Say, Doc," the patient asked, "haven't you ever seen a cat?"

Stout Lady: I'm putting on too much weight, Doctor. What shall I do?
Doctor: I prescribe regular exercise. Just push yourself away from the table
 three times a day.

Nurse: Shall we boil the instruments, Doctor?
Doctor: No, let's *fry* them today!

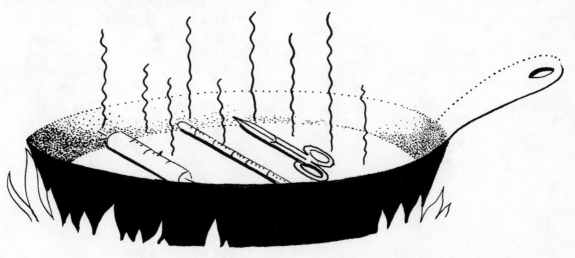

SCHOOL DAYS

Teacher: Billy, you missed school yesterday, didn't you?
Billy: Not a bit!

Student: This isn't fair! I don't think I deserve an absolute ZERO!
Teacher: Neither do I, but it's the lowest mark I can give.

Teacher: Did you write this poem without any help?
Student: I did.
Teacher: Then I'm very pleased to meet you, Lord Tennyson. I thought you had died years ago!

Teacher: What do you expect to be when you get out of school?
Pupil: An old man.

Teacher: George, can you give me Lincoln's Gettysburg Address?
George: No, but he used to live at the White House in Washington.

Teacher: Why don't you answer me?
Willie: I did. I shook my head.
Teacher: You don't expect me to hear it rattle way up here, do you?

Teacher: Give, for one year, the number of tons of coal shipped out of
    the United States.
Pupil: 1492 — none.

Teacher: Peter, name two pronouns.
Peter: Who, me?
Teacher: That's correct.

As the first grade's drawing period came to a close, the teacher went about the room to inspect her pupils' art work. At one of the tables, she found Jimmy's picture of a stagecoach, which was lacking in one important feature — it had no wheels.

"Your picture is very well done, so far as it goes," said the teacher encouragingly, "but there are no wheels on the stagecoach. What holds it up?"

The little artist smiled. "Bad guys," he answered knowingly.

The principal gazed sternly at the problem child who had been sent to his office. "This is the fifth time you've been in here this week," he said. "Now, what have you to say for yourself?"

"I'm sure glad it's Friday."

Teacher: Did your father help you with this problem?
Pupil: No, I got it wrong by myself.

I'll never forget the time I went to school. What fun I had that day!
That day? You only went to school for one day?
Why, are you supposed to go back?

(Little boy, saying prayer): God bless Ma and Pa and make Youngstown the capital of Ohio.
Mother: Why?
Little boy: Because that's what I put on my examination paper.

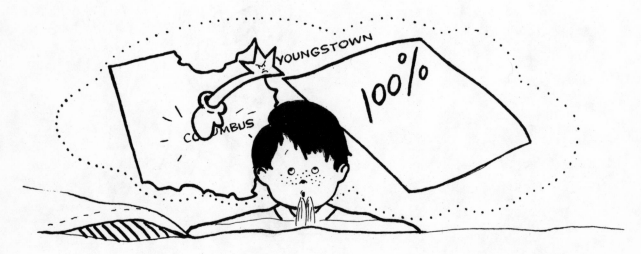

Teacher: Can you tell me where elephants are found?

Willie: Elephants, teacher, are so big they are hardly ever lost.

The teacher told the class to write a composition on baseball. One minute later, little Johnny turned in his written effort. It read, "Game called on account of rain."

The kindergarten teacher looked about the room. All of her charges seemed to be busy at one activity or another — stringing beads, folding and pasting paper, and drawing and coloring pictures — with the exception of one little boy who simply sat in his chair doing nothing.

Coming up to him, the teacher inquired, "Are you free, Harold?"

"No," replied Harold brightly. "I'm five!"

INVENTIONS

I've invented something which will allow people to see through walls.
Wonderful! What are you going to call it?
A window.

I've invented a piano without any keys, strings, pedals or legs.
What would you call that?
Nothing.

What's this peculiar key on your typewriter? I have never seen it on any
    other typewriter before.
It's my own invention. Whenever I can't spell a word, I hit this key and
    it makes a blur.

Once upon a time, a man invented a tonic that could put hair on a billiard
ball. But he died in poverty, because no one wanted to buy a billiard ball with
hair on it.

A cellophane newspaper, so that wives may see their husbands over the
breakfast table.

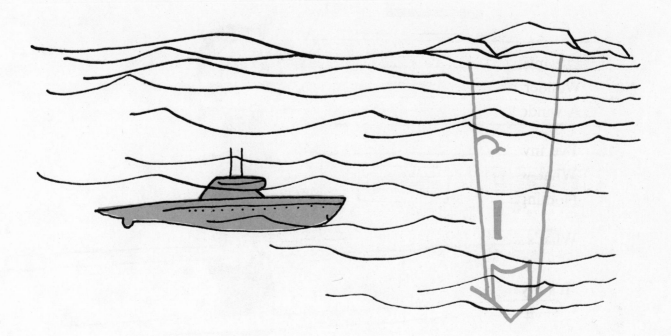

An inverted lighthouse, for submarines.

A pencil with rubber lead, for people who may want to stretch a point.

A cuckoo clock where the cuckoo comes out and asks, "What time is it?"

Neon thumbs for night hitchhikers.

A lamp with no bulbs, for people who like to sit in the dark.

A hollow chisel, for talking through to get a word in edgewise.

An automobile without a horn, for people who don't give a hoot.

A round hole cut in a door, for circular letters.

A perfumed bookmark. If it slips down into the book, just sniff along the edge to find your place.

A shotgun with one barrel on top of the other instead of side by side — for shooting ducks that happen to be riding piggyback.

A stepladder without steps on it, for washing windows in the basement.

A fish hook with a camera on it, to take a picture of the one that got away.

A cookbook full of blank pages, for writing down the names and addresses of good restaurants.

A toaster with knives on its sides that scrape the toast after it pops out.

A car with no wheels. It saves money; just leave it in the garage and ride a bicycle.

Bread with wires in it, for people who have no toaster. All that needs to be done is plug in the bread.

An alarm clock with half a bell on it, for awakening only one of two people who are sleeping in the same room.

DOPEY DOINGS

I saw you pushing your bicycle along the street yesterday.
Yes, I was late for an appointment and didn't have time to get on.

Mopey: How would you like a pair of book ends for Christmas?
Dopey: Oh, that would be fine — I always read the end of the book
before the beginning.

Silly No. 1: What do they do with the leftover holes in doughnuts?
Silly No. 2: They tie them up with string and make fish nets.

What time is it?
Five o'clock?
How do you like that? I've been asking people all day what time it is
and everybody tells me something different.

Did you sleep well last night?
No, the sheep couldn't jump the fence and they kept landing on me.

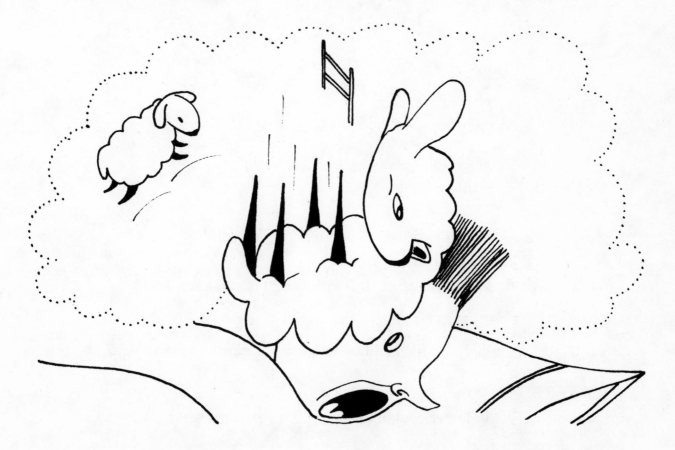

I had to sell my alarm clock last week.
For goodness' sake, why?
It kept going off while I was asleep.

Why do you put your money under the mattress?
So that I'll have something to fall back on.

This match won't light.
What's the matter with it?
I don't know — it lit all right last night.

Billy: If you lost your dog, why don't you put an ad in the paper?
Silly: There's no point in that. My dog can't read!

My feet are sticking out of the covers and they're cold!
Well, why don't you pull them in?
What! Have those icy things in bed with me? I should say not!

Did you send the letter air mail?
Yes. And I put a light on the mailbox to show the plane where to land.

Tell me, why are you so half-baked?
It's a sad story. My father couldn't keep up the payments on the incubator.

He was caught cheating in astronomy class.
Really? How?
Well, the teacher asked him to describe the stars and he began hitting
    himself on the head.

Why do you wear that toothbrush in your lapel?
It's my boy friend's class pin — he went to Colgate.

How do you spell Mississippi?
The river or the state?

Did you put new water in the fish bowl?
I didn't have to. The fish haven't drunk what was in it yet.

You look kind of blue. What's the matter with you?
It's just that I forget to breathe every once in a while.

You have your boots on the wrong feet.
Well, they're the only feet I have!

Teacher: Why are you late this morning?

Johnny: I squeezed the toothpaste too hard and it took me half an hour to get it back into the tube.

I'd like some DDT, please.

How do you spell it?

Voice on telephone: Is this 1-5-1-5?

Dopey: No, this is fifteen-fifteen.

Voice on telephone: Sorry to have bothered you.

Dopey: Oh, that's all right. I had to answer the phone anyway.

Why don't you answer the phone?

It isn't ringing.

Must you always wait till the last moment?

I'm glad I'm not a bird. I might get hurt.

Why?

I can't fly.

Do you know that I weighed only four pounds when I was born?

Did you live?

You should see me now!

Do you use toothpaste?

Why, no — none of my teeth are loose!

Ow-eee! I just scalded my hand in the hot water.

Why don't you feel the water before you put your hand in it?

First Sportsman: If a flock of birds came into sight and went "Honk, honk!" what would you do?
Second Sportsman: I'd get out of their way.

What are those things floating in the water?
Jellyfish.
What flavor?

Who are you writing to?
Myself.
What does your letter say?
How should I know? I haven't received it yet.

I'm not feeling well today. I ate a dozen oysters last night.
Were they fresh? What did they look like when you opened them?
Oh, do you have to open them?

Do fish perspire?
Naturally. What do you think makes the sea salty?

How do you spell "imbecile?"
I-m-b-e-s-s-e-l-l.
The dictionary spells it i-m-b-e-c-i-l-e.
You didn't ask me how the dictionary spelled it — you asked me how *I* spelled it.

Does your watch tell the time?
No — you have to look at it.

SILLIES

Why did the silly tiptoe past the medicine cabinet?

He didn't want to wake up the sleeping pills.

Why did the silly jump out of an airplane?

He just wanted to try out his new spring suit.

Why didn't the silly return a borrowed book?

Because he was a bookkeeper.

Why did the silly take a ladder to school?

Because he wanted to go to high school.

Why did the silly sleep in front of the fire?

Because he wanted to sleep like a log.

Why did the silly put his father in the refrigerator?

Because he wanted a cold pop.

Why did the thin silly jump out of the window?

Because he wanted to come down plump.

Why did the silly's wife knit him three stockings?

Because he had written her, saying he had grown another foot.

Why did the silly keep running around his bed?

He wanted to catch up on his sleep.

Why did the silly eat dynamite?

He wanted his hair to grow out in bangs.

Why did the silly drive his new car off the cliff?

He wanted to try out his air brakes.

Why did the silly take a cigarette out of the box?

To make it a cigarette lighter.

Why did the silly throw a pumpkin into the air?

So that it would come down squash.

CAUGHT YOU!

I've just returned from a safari in Africa.
How was the hunting?
Not bad. I bagged some lions, a leopard and a potfor.
What's a potfor?
To cook in, silly!

Do you know the difference between taxis and buses?
No.
Good. We'll take a bus.

Larry: I have a car that has no engine and no wheels. All it has is a horn.
Harry: How does it go?
Larry: BEEP! BEEP!

What's the difference between a lemon and a head of cabbage?
I don't know.
You'd be a fine one to send out after lemons!

I'll have you know that everyone in my block looks to me for advice
and follows it!
I don't doubt it. You're a natural-born blockhead.

Have you time for a couple of dillies?
Yes.
Dilly, dilly!

Do you believe in free speech?
Why, of course!
Good! Mind if I use your telephone?

I guess I'm the black sheep of my family.
You must be, you muttonhead.

Silly: Have you met my parents?
Billy: No, I haven't.
Silly (holding out his hand): Well, meet my paw!

I'm a self-made man.
That's what I like about you. You always take the blame for everything.

Do you know the story about the three eggs?
No.
Two bad!

Why is a crow?
I don't know. Why?
Caws!

Do you know what they call watermelons in Louisiana?
No! What?
Watermelons.

You know, it's easy to make a cigarette lighter.
Really? How?
Remove all of the tobacco!

What three words do ignorant people speak most often?
I don't know.
That's right.

Gonna be tough sleddin' today.
How come?
No snow.

Have you heard the joke about the roof?
No, I haven't.
Well, it's over your head.

I've changed my mind.
Thank goodness! Does it work better now?

Did you hear the story about the peacock?
No, I didn't.
It's a beautiful tale.

Which is correct: The white of eggs *is* yellow, or the white of eggs *are* yellow?
Neither. (The whites are certainly not yellow!)

What's the difference between a mailbox on a street corner and a kangaroo's pouch?
I don't know.
Remind me not to have you mail my letters. You might drop them in a kangaroo's pouch.

I took lessons from a correspondence school once.
You must have lost most of your mail.

Who's that homely man sitting over there?
That's my brother.
Oh, I'm sorry. I didn't notice the resemblance.

Isn't it great to be alive?
Yes, I feel better that way, too.

ABSENT-MINDEDNESS

Wife: The doctor's here, dear.
Absent-minded Man: Tell him I can't see him. I'm sick.

Barber: If you want a haircut, would you mind taking your hat off?
Absent-minded Man: Oh, I didn't realize there were ladies present.

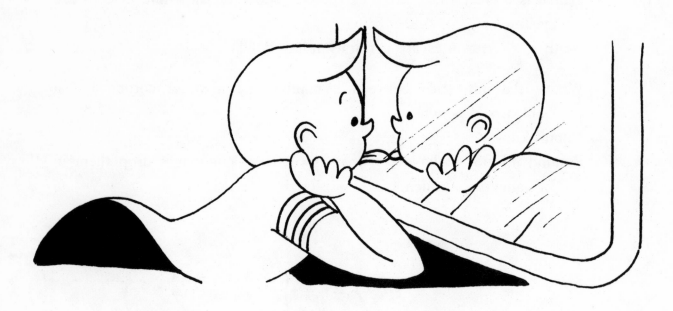

Pete is terribly absent-minded. He once stood in front of a mirror for two hours trying to remember where he had seen himself before.

The absent-minded farmer suddenly realized that he had a rope in his hand. "Now, I wonder," he mused, "have I found a piece of rope or lost a horse?"

Professor: I hate to mention it, dear, but the toast is quite tough.
Wife: That's the cork mat you're eating, dear.

Ned: Oh, I see you've put on your long winter underwear.
Ed: How in the world did you know?
Ned: You forgot to put on your pants.

A man was so absent-minded that he put his dog to bed and let himself out the back door. He didn't discover his mistake until next morning, when he chased a cow and found that he couldn't bark.

A farmer was so absent-minded that he started out after his cow, found a cowbell in the road, pocketed it, and followed its tinkle for fifteen miles before he remembered it was not on the cow's neck.

"Is is true, sir, that professors are absent-minded?" a student asked a college professor one day.

"Nonsense!" replied the professor. "Professors haven't got bad memories. Don't you think I know where I am right now? And don't you think I'll know tomorrow where I was today? The whole thing is a complete fallacy. Now, are there any other questions?"

Another student stood up. "Is it true," he asked, "that professors are absent-minded and have bad memories?"

"Now I had an idea that sooner or later someone would ask me that question," began the professor. "It's utter nonsense . . ."

Wife: Why did you cut out the back part of that book?

Absent-minded Doctor: Oh, my! It was marked "Appendix" and I took it out without thinking!

HERE, THERE AND EVERYWHERE

At Albuquerque, New Mexico, a tourist was introduced to an Indian who had a reputation for an astonishing memory. Thinking to test him, the tourist put his first question to the Indian: "What did you have for breakfast on December 16, 1948?"

"Eggs!" replied the Indian, without a moment's hesitation.

The tourist scoffed. "Everyone eats eggs for breakfast," he mumbled. "He's a fraud."

Eight years later the tourist happened to pass through Albuquerque again and he saw the same Indian lounging on the station platform. Jovially, the tourist approached the Indian and said, "How!"

And the Indian promptly answered, "Scrambled!"

An airplane containing the pilot and his only passenger were circling high above a small flying field. Suddenly the pilot cut his motor and began gliding.

"Know what?" chuckled the pilot as he looked down. "I'll bet half of the people down there right now think we're going to crash."

The passenger gulped nervously. "Half of us up here do, too," he said.

A man was once known to be so polite at all times that when he passed a hen on her nest, he tipped his hat and said, "Please don't get up, ma'am."

I suppose you met a lot of Greeks while you were in Athens.
Yes, they have them over there, too.

Tourist: I've come here for the winter.
Californian: Well, you've come to the wrong place. There's no winter here.

What do they call all the little rivers that run into the Nile?
The juveniles.

How do they estimate the population of a Swiss village?
They count the echoes and divide by the number of mountains.

Do you know that Eskimos exist mainly on whale meat and blubber?
Well, you'd cry, too, if you had only whale meat to eat.

Policeman: The signs all say, "Speed limit, 15 miles an hour."
Motorist: But officer, how could I read them when I was going over 50?

The woman who had just gotten on the bus handed the bus driver a brand-new five-dollar bill. "I'm sorry I don't have any dimes for the fare," she said apologetically.

"Don't worry," said the bus driver, reaching for his change-maker. "You'll have fifty of them in a minute."

Is he a worldly man?

I'd say so. He's larger at the equator than at the poles.

A woman walked into a bank and presented a check for cashing.

"Please endorse this," the teller said.

The woman returned a moment later.

The teller looked at the back of the check. It read, "I heartily endorse this."

Postal Clerk: Madam, you've put too much postage on this letter.

Old Lady: Oh, mercy! I hope it won't go too far!

Say, what's the death rate around here?

Same as everywhere, bub — one to a person.

Missionary: Do your people know anything about religion?

Cannibal Chief: We had a taste of it when the last missionary was here.

Customs Inspector: What have you to declare?

Traveler: I declare, I'm glad to get back home.

Wife: There! That does it — the car is parked.

Husband: It's close enough. We can walk to the curb.

Lady of the House: Can you prove that you worked for the Updykes?
Maid: Well, I can show you some spoons with their initials on them.

If a lion were stalking you, what steps would you take?
The longest steps I could!

Mayor: How do you like our city?
Indian Visitor: Very well, thank you. How do you like our country?

A little girl came into a grocery store and said, "My Mommy told me to tell you that we found a dead fly in the raisin bread."

"All right," replied the clerk behind the counter. "Tell you what I'll do — bring me in the fly and I'll give you a raisin."

"Company, atten-shun!" bawled the drill sergeant to the awkward squad. "Lift up your left leg and hold it straight out in front of you."

The squad obeyed the unusual order without question, but by mistake, one rookie held up his right leg, which brought it out side by side with his neighbor's left leg.

"All right, all right," shouted the hard-boiled sergeant. "Who's the wise guy over there holding up *both* legs?"

Lady of the House: Has the canary had its bath?
Maid: Yes, ma'am. You can come in now.

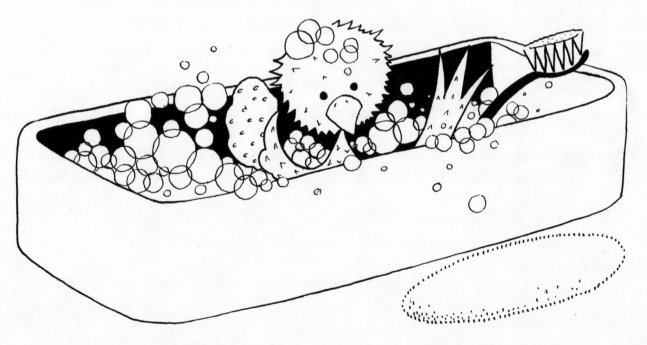

You'd better go a little slower — you're doing 70 miles an **hour**.
Imagine that! And I only learned how to drive yesterday!

Does your wife know how to park a car?
Well, she doesn't exactly park a car — she abandons it.

Son: Come on, Dad. Buy a new car.
Dad: Wait until I've had a ride in the old one first, will you?

Tourist: How large a fire do you build for smoke signals?
Modern Indian: It all depends on whether it's a local or a long-distance call.

Customer: What makes the car jerk so when I first put it into gear?
Used-car Salesman: Eagerness to get away, sir — nothing more.

Hey, you — you're blocking traffic. Can't you go any faster?
Yes, but I don't want to leave the car.

Wife: It's Washington's Birthday, so I baked you a cherry pie.
Husband: All right, bring me a hatchet so I can cut it.

I wish I could stop my wife from spending so much money for gloves.
Buy her a diamond ring.

Boarder: Does the water always come through the roof like this?
Landlord: No — only when it rains.

Wife: How many times have I told you not to be late for dinner?
Husband: I don't know. I thought you were keeping score.

That's a terrible picture of me. It makes me look as fat as a hippopotamus!
You should have thought of that before you had it taken, dear.

What's the smudge on your face?
Smudge? Oh, well, I just left my wife at the railroad station where I kissed
    her good-by.
But how did you get the smudge?
After I kissed her, I ran up front to kiss the engine!

Mr. Penny (to butler): Please announce Mr. and Mrs. Penny and daughter.
Butler (loudly): Three cents!

Maid: The oil stove has gone out, ma'am.
Lady of the House: Well, light it again.
Maid: But I can't — it has gone out through the roof!

Wife: I'm going to enter this contest. They're giving wonderful prizes for the best ways of completing a sentence in 25 words or less.

Husband: I'll give you a prize, myself, if you can finish *any* sentence in 25 words or less!

Junior: Shall I mail this letter for you, Mommy?

Mother: No, I wouldn't send a dog out in weather like this. Let your father go out and mail it.

I'm on my way to visit my outlaws.

You mean your in-laws, don't you?

No — outlaws. They're a bunch of bandits.

Could you direct me to the First National Bank?

Yes — for a dollar.

A dollar! Isn't that asking too much?

Not for a bank director.

Eskimo Boy: I would push my dog team a thousand miles through ice and snow just to tell you that I love you.

Eskimo Girl: That's a lot of mush!

Lady of the House: If the master brings home some friends for dinner, will you be prepared?
Cook: Yes, ma'am — my bag is already packed.

Did you stay at that hotel very long?
No, just long enough to hear their rates, that's all.

Judge: The charges against you are that you ran over this man, and also speeding.
Motorist: Yes, your Honor — I was hurrying to get over him.

Pardon me, does this train stop at Little Junction?
Yes — just watch me and get off one station before I do.

I once carried a hundred-pound load on my back for a mile.
I'll bet it got heavier with every step, didn't it?
No — it was ice.

Hostess: When you serve my guests tonight, please don't wear any jewelry.
Maid: I haven't anything valuable, ma'am, but thanks for the warning.

Is it bad luck to have a cat follow you?
That depends — are you a man or a mouse?

Day after day, the boy and his dog went to school together.
But one day they were separated.
The dog graduated.

A woman leaving a self-service automatic elevator asked an incoming passenger, "What's that 'pass' button for?" She pointed to a button on the panel inside the car.

"That's so you can go by some floors without stopping," was the reply.

"Oh," said the woman. "I *wondered* how one elevator could pass another!"

Mack: I was once a 90-pound weakling. When I went to the beach a 200-pound bully kicked sand in my face. That did it. I exercised hard every day — and in a little while I, too, weighed 200 pounds.

Jack: Then what happened?

Mack: I went to the beach and a 400-pound bully kicked sand in my face!

When Jimmy's pet canary died, his father supplied an empty cigarette carton for the bird, and with much ceremony buried it in a corner of the garden.

"Daddy, do you think my canary will go to Heaven?" Jimmy asked as they walked back to the house.

"Sure, he will," replied the father reassuringly.

"I was only thinking," murmured Jimmy, "that God might be disappointed when he opens the box and doesn't find any cigarettes in it."

Mrs. Jones: George, wake up — I hear a mouse squeaking.

Mr. Jones: I'll oil it first thing in the morning.

Barber: Sir, would you mind turning the other side of your face toward me?
Customer: Oh, are you through shaving this side?
Barber: No, but I can't stand the sight of blood.

Did you know that Nancy married a janitor?
No. How did it happen?
He just swept her off her feet.

Motorist: Remember that car you sold me two weeks ago?
Used-car Dealer: Yes.
Motorist: Tell me again all you said about it then. I'm getting discouraged.

It will take me a long time to forget you.
About how long?
I beg your pardon — have we met?

Doctor: Are you taking good care of that cold?
Patient: I certainly am. I've had it a full month and it's just as good as new.

Doctor, come at once! Our baby has swallowed a fountain pen!
I'll be right over. What are you doing in the meantime?
Using a pencil.

Lady of the House: Will you call me early in the morning, Nora?

Nora: Certainly, ma'am — just ring me.

Maid (to Lady of the House): While you were gone, ma'am, your little Ambrose swallowed a bug. But don't worry — I had him take some insect powder.

Lady of the House: Kate, did you wash this fish carefully before you baked it?

Kate: Now wouldn't that be silly? What's the use of washing a fish that's lived all its life in water?

Butler: I have grown gray in your service and now I'm dismissed. Is there nothing you can do for me?

Master: Yes, you may take my bottle of hair dye when you go.

Bakery Clerk: Here's a very nice cake — I'm sure you'll like it.

Customer: Umm-m, I don't know. That cake looks as if the mice had been eating it.

Bakery Clerk: Impossible. The cat has been lying on it all night.

The Persian Gulf is the hottest place in the world. Fishes have been seen swimming about with their heads out of the water and the perspiration streaming off their faces.

Housewife: I'm sorry, sir, but my husband and I have made it a policy never to buy anything from door-to-door salesmen.

Salesman: Then I have the very thing for you, ma'am. I'm sure you will not want to be without one of these handsome "No Salesmen" signs.

Mother: Danny's teacher says he ought to have an encyclopedia.
Father: Let him walk to school like I did.

Judge: The last time I saw you, I told you that I didn't want to see you here again!
Prisoner: That's what I tried to tell these policemen, your Honor, but they wouldn't believe me.

Whenever my wife needs money, she calls me handsome.
Handsome?
Yes — hand some over.

The wealthy Texas oil man was greeted one evening by his young son who announced happily, "Daddy, I sold my dog today."
"Sold your dog?" asked the father. "For how much?"
"A thousand dollars."
"Really? Let me see the money."
"Oh, I didn't get any money," replied the son. "I got two five-hundred-dollar cats for it."

Can you carry a tune?
Certainly.
Well, carry the one you're whistling out in the back yard and bury it.

Do you run a car?
No, I let the engine do that.

Yes, I once got ten dollars a word.
How was that?
I talked back to the judge.

He: You look good enough to eat.
She: I do eat. Where shall we go?

There was a young lady named Bright
Whose speed was much faster than light.
    She set out one day
    In a relative way,
And returned on the previous night.

Did the doctor treat you yesterday?
No, he charged me ten dollars.

I have a very nice apartment for you.
By the week or by the month?
By the incinerator.

How big is this ice rink?
It seats 2000.

A cheerful old bear at the zoo
Could always find something to do.
    When it bored him, you know,
    To walk to and fro,
He reversed it and walked fro and to.

You drive awfully fast, don't you?
Yes, I hit 70 yesterday.
Did you kill any of them?

I just got a job at the Eagle Laundry.
What do you do there?
Wash eagles, of course!

COURT SHORTS

Judge: Order! Order in the court!

Prisoner: Ham and cheese on rye, please.

Judge: If this trial is interrupted by anyone, that person will be thrown right out of this courtroom.

Prisoner: Hooray for the judge!

Prosecutor: What were you doing on July 15th at 9 o'clock in the evening?

Prisoner: I was eating a hamburger.

Prosecutor: What were you doing at 9:30?

Prisoner: I was taking bicarbonate of soda.

Prosecutor: Do you expect us to believe that?

Prisoner: You would if you had eaten one of those hamburgers.

Prisoner: All I want is justice!

Judge: I'd like to help you, but all I can give you is ten years.

Woman: Your Honor, the accident was unavoidable. I had to run into the fence to keep from hitting the cow.

Judge: Was it a Jersey cow?

Woman: I don't know — I didn't see any license plates.

DINNER IS SERVED

Waiter (to man who has just had his seventh bowl of soup): You must be very fond of soup, sir.

Diner: Yes, indeed — or I wouldn't be drinking so much water to get so little.

Didn't anyone ever tell you that it's impolite to read at the table?

Yes.

Well, stop looking so intently at your alphabet soup!

Waiter: Sir, we are famous for snails here.

Diner: I thought so. I've been served by one already.

Diner: Waiter, there's a bit of canvas in my fish.

Waiter: Why not? It's a sailfish.

Diner: Waiter, have you ever been to the zoo?

Waiter: No, sir.

Diner: Well, you ought to go. You'd enjoy seeing the turtles whizzing by.

Diner: Waiter, your thumb is on my steak. Remove it this instant.

Waiter: What, and drop it again?

Diner: I can't eat this stuff — call the manager.

Waiter: It's no use — he won't eat it either.

Waiter: Aren't you the same man who complained last week?
Diner: No — after that meal, I'll never be the same.

There was no spoon with the cup of coffee served the diner. "It's going to be pretty hot to stir this coffee with my finger," said the diner jokingly.

A minute later the waiter reappeared at the table with another cup of coffee. "Maybe this isn't so hot, sir," he said.

Diner: Waiter, your thumb is in my soup.
Waiter: That's all right. It's so used to the heat I hardly noticed it.

Diner: Waiter, I think my soup is cold.
Waiter: Well, make up your mind — this restaurant can't be bothered with rumors.

Feeling hungry and despondent, a man walked into a diner and said to the waitress who came up to take his order, "I would like some stew, if you please — and a few kind words."

The waitress went away for a few minutes and then returned with a plate of stew which she set before the customer.

"That's part of my order, all right," said the man, smiling. "Now, do you have a few kind words?"

"Yes," whispered the waitress, "don't eat the stew!"

Why do you eat in cafeterias?
The doctor said I should take long walks before meals.

Diner: Are you the lad who took my order?
Waiter: Yes, sir.
Diner: Bless me, how you've grown!

Waiter: Our chef made pies long before you were born.
Patron: That's when he must have baked this one.

Waiter: How did you find the steak, sir?
Diner: By accident. I moved the potato aside and there it was.

Diner: I would like some oysters. Don't make them too cold. Not too
　　large. Not too young nor too old. And I want them right away.
Waiter: Yes, sir. Do you want them with or without pearls?

Look here, waiter, is this peach or apple pie?
Can't you tell from the taste?
No, I can't.
Well, then, what difference does it make?

Diner: Well, waiter, what's on the menu today?
Waiter: Everything, sir.
Diner: Bring me everything. Have it served at once.
Waiter (shouting to cook): One order of hash!

Diner: Waiter, there's a tack in my doughnut.
Waiter: Why, the ambitious thing! He must have thought it was a tire.

Waiter: George Washington once dined at this very table.
Diner: Is that why you haven't changed the tablecloth since?

Diner: Take back this steak. I've been trying to cut it for ten minutes, but it's so tough I can't even make a dent in it.
Waiter: I'm sorry, sir, but I can't take it back. You've bent it.

There's something wrong with this chicken a la king.
There can't be — the cookbook says it's perfectly delicious.

Waiter: If you order a fresh egg here, you get the freshest egg in the world. If you order a good cup of coffee, you get the best cup of coffee in the world, and . . .
Diner: I believe you. I ordered a small steak.

How long can you use a tea bag?
Indefinitely — as long as you keep using rusty water.

Do you want your eggs turned over?
Yes, turn them over to the Museum of Natural History.

Patron: Waiter, this piece of fish isn't nearly as good as the piece of fish I had here last week.
Waiter: That's funny — it's off the same fish.

Eating, hey?
No, it's spaghetti.

Customer: What are these pennies doing in my soup?

Waiter: Well, sir, you said you'd stop eating here if there wasn't some change in your meals.

This goulash is terrible.

That's funny. I put a brand new pair of goulashes in it.

Waiter, there's a fly in my soup!

1. That will be ten cents extra, please.
2. I've been looking for him all day.
3. What do you expect with the blue plate — a hummingbird?
4. That's all right — he won't drink much.
5. All right, I'll bring you a fork.
6. Ah, cornered at last!
7. That's strange — what kind of soup is it?
8. Yes, we ran out of turtles.

How do foreign dishes compare with American ones?

Oh, they break just as easily.

With which hand do you eat mashed potatoes?

My right hand.

I always use a fork.

ANIMAL ANTICS

A lion was walking through a jungle one day, feeling mean. The first animal he chanced to meet was a monkey.

"Who is King of the Jungle?" he roared, grabbing the hapless monkey with a powerful paw.

"You are, oh mighty lion," replied the trembling monkey.

The lion released the monkey and then came upon a tiger. "Who is King of the Jungle?" he roared again.

"You are, oh mighty lion," was the tiger's answer.

Then the lion met an elephant, to whom the same question was put: "Who is King of the Jungle?"

Without a word, the elephant grabbed the lion with his trunk, whirled him about, and threw him to the ground.

"Just because you don't know the answer," mumbled the subdued lion as he managed to rise slowly, "is no reason for you to get so rough!"

Animals are smarter than humans. Put fifteen horses in a race and thousands of people go to see it. But put fifteen people in a race and not one horse would go to see it.

Mother Pigeon (to son): "Watch your posture — you're beginning to walk people-toed!"

"How will you have your beef today?" asked the zoo attendant.
"O-O-O — W-O-W — O-O-O!" returned the lion so loudly that the windows shook.
And then the attendant knew that he wanted it *roar*.

Mother and Father Kangaroo were on their way to a picnic one day, but every once in a while Baby Kangaroo kept popping out of his mother's pouch. At length Father Kangaroo became impatient and said to his wife, "Why don't you tuck the little one farther down into your pouch so that he won't keep popping out?"
"It isn't his fault," replied Mother Kangaroo. "It's just that I have hiccups!"

What's your cat's name?
Ben Hur.
How did you happen to call it that?
Well, we called it Ben until it had kittens.

An elephant never forgets — but, after all, what has an elephant got to remember?

A man and his dog sat in a theater, obviously enjoying a movie. When it ended, the dog applauded until his paws were sore.
At this sight, a nearby spectator expressed his amazement. "Most astounding!" he exclaimed.
"Yes, it is," agreed the dog owner. "Rover hated the book, you know!"

Mrs. Greenbottle Fly: How's the new baby?
Mrs. Bluebottle Fly: Very restless. I had to walk the ceiling with him all night!

Tim Turtle: I can't think of what I ought to get my wife for her birthday. Do you have any suggestions?
Tom Turtle: Why not a people-necked sweater?

First Dragon: Am I late for supper?
Second Dragon: Yes — everyone's eaten.

A snake snapped at me.
Snakes don't snap — they coil and strike.
This one was a garter snake.

Barracuda: What's that two-legged thing that just fell into the water?
Shark: I don't know, but I'll bite.

Old Hen: Let me give you some advice
Young Hen: Yes, what is it?
Old Hen: An egg a day keeps the ax away.

A man bought a horse from a farmer one day and was just about to ride off in the wagon to which the horse was hitched up when the farmer spoke up. "I think I should mention this," he said. "That horse you just bought has a very peculiar habit — he likes to sit on eggs."

"He likes to *what?*" asked the man incredulously.

"He likes to sit on eggs," repeated the farmer. "I've tried to break him of the habit, but it's no use. He just takes a notion to sit on eggs whenever he sees any around."

"Well, I need a horse," said the man, "so I guess I'll just have to watch to see that there are no eggs nearby." And he drove away.

It wasn't long before they passed a farm, and as luck would have it, there was a henhouse in plain view, as were also dozens of nice, fresh eggs. Before the man could even become aware of the situation, the horse trotted up to a nestful of white eggs and plumped himself down on it.

The man got out of his wagon and then, only after numerous tuggings and words ranging from coaxings to threats, led the horse out of sight of the eggs. Soon they were going along again as if nothing had happened. But then, just as they came alongside a small brook, the horse suddenly turned without warning, waded into the middle of the stream, and sat down again!

The man became quite angry. Leaving the horse and wagon just as they were in the water, he made his way to the nearest telephone and called up the farmer.

"That horse you sold me — the one who likes to sit on eggs . . ." began the man.

"What about him?" asked the farmer.

"Right now that silly nag is sitting down in the middle of a stream!" said the man.

"Oh, I forgot to tell you," the farmer replied, "he likes to sit on *fish* too!"

There was once a nearsighted snake who fell in love with a rope.

Mother Kangaroo was puzzled. She kept scratching in and out of the pouch where her two little youngsters were. Finally she realized what was happening. She reached into the pouch and pulled out the two little kangaroos. Then she set them on the ground and spanked them both soundly with her tail.

"There!" she said. "That will teach you to eat crackers in bed!"

How can you trail an elephant in the jungle?
By the faint odor of peanuts on its breath.

A guinea pig was talking to another guinea pig in his cage at the research laboratory. "You know," he said, "I think I've got Dr. Benson conditioned."

"Really?" said the second guinea pig. "What makes you think so?"

"Well," said the first guinea pig, "every time I go through the maze and ring the bell he gives me food."

Once upon a time there were two skunks named In and Out.
When In was out, Out was in. When Out was out, In would be in.
One day Out was in and In was out. Mother Skunk, who was in with Out, said, "Out, I want you to go out and bring In in." And in two shakes of a tail, Out did go out and brought In in.

"How did you find In so quickly?" Mother Skunk asked.

"It was easy," said Out. "Instinct!"

COMEDY OF ERRORS

Electrician: Your doorbell doesn't work, lady, because you have a short circuit in the wiring.
Housewife: Well, for goodness' sake, lengthen it!

You're supposed to eat a balanced diet.
That's what this is. Every bean weighs the same.

Do these stairs take you to the third floor?
No, you'll have to walk.

A cowboy walked into the ranch house wearing a large, flashing diamond ring on his finger.
"Is that a real diamond?" his friends asked.
"If it ain't," replied the cowboy, "I've been cheated out of a dollar and a half."

Do you believe in clubs for young people?
Only when kindness fails.

Cowhand: Aren't you putting that saddle on backward, sir?
Dude: That's all you know about it, buster. You don't even know which way I'm going.

A bank teller was given a package of dollar bills with instructions to count them, in order to make sure that there were 100.

He started his check and got as far as 58 in his count. Then he threw the package down. "If it's right this far," he said, "it's probably right all the way."

Why don't you buy Christmas seals?
Oh, I really don't know how I'd feed them!

Landlady (to tenant who has been keeping everyone awake with his piano playing): Hey, don't you know there's an old lady sick upstairs?
Musician: No, but if you'll hum the tune, I can play it by ear.

Don't interrupt me while I'm in conversation.
Oh, I'm sorry — I thought you were only talking.

Remember that piano stool you sold me?
Yes.
Well, I twisted it in all directions, but I can't get a single note out of it.

Passing through a small old-fashioned village one warm summer day, a group of hikers decided to rest a bit.

Just as they were ready to move on again, one man, nearly out of breath, came running up and shouted, "Hey, fellers! I just saw a man building a horse. Come look! He's nailing on the back feet now."

Executive: Get me the toy department.
Secretary: Any particular toy you'd like to speak to?

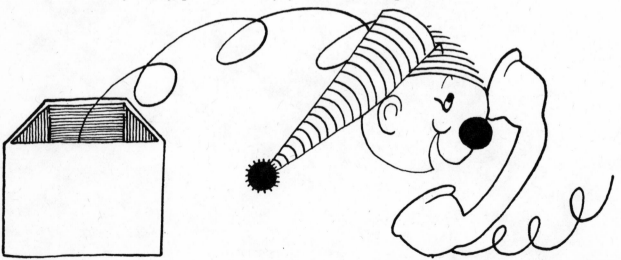

Old Lady: Must I stick the stamp on myself?
Post Office Employee: No, stick it on the envelope.

I just had my appendix removed.
Have a scar?
No, thanks, I don't smoke.

Don't you like music?
I certainly do. I have a zither at home.
Really? I have a brother at home.
No, you don't understand. A zither is a sort of lyre.
Well, my brother is a liar.

Examining a check presented to him for cashing, the bank teller asked the woman who had given it to him, "Can you identify yourself?"

Instantly she opened her purse and pulled out a small mirror. "Yes," she said, after glancing in it for a moment, "it's me all right!"

A man once bought a valuable vase in China. He brought it to his home and there it was an object of admiration and conversation for years. But one day it fell off its pedestal and cracked. And so the man immediately sent it back to the maker in China with orders that it be duplicated exactly.

It took some time. Six years later, he received the vase back — plus a perfect replica, right down to the jagged crack.

How did you like the bath salts, madam?

They're very good-tasting, but a real bath is ever so much better.

I'd like to have that fellow's scalp!

Why? Are you mad at him?

No, mine is full of dandruff.

Landlady: A professor once had this room. He invented an explosive

New Roomer: Oh! I suppose those spots on the ceiling are the explosive.

Landlady: No, that's the professor!

It's too bad that he always takes the worst possible view of everything.

He's a pessimist, I take it.

No — an amateur photographer.

Do you know that Wally beats his brother up every morning?

How awful!

Yes. He gets up at seven, and his brother gets up at eight.

Fred: I wish I had enough money to buy an elephant.

Ned: Whatever do you want an elephant for?

Fred: I don't. I just wish I had that much money.

Riding Instructor: What kind of saddle do you want — one with a horn or one without?

Dude: Without, I guess. There doesn't seem to be much traffic around here.

How many miles per hour can this boat go?

This boat doesn't go miles — it goes knots.

With all the boats around, *we* had to pick one that goes knots!

Theater manager: Madam, you may not take that dog into the theater — it is not permitted.

Woman: Absurd! What harm could the movies do to a little dog like this?

Do you like codfish balls?

I don't know — I've never been to one.

Jim: I failed my first-aid test in the Boy Scouts.

Tim: Why?

Jim: I tried to bandage a hiccup!

I fell over twenty feet today.

My goodness! Were you hurt?

Oh, no — I was just moving down the aisle on a crowded bus.

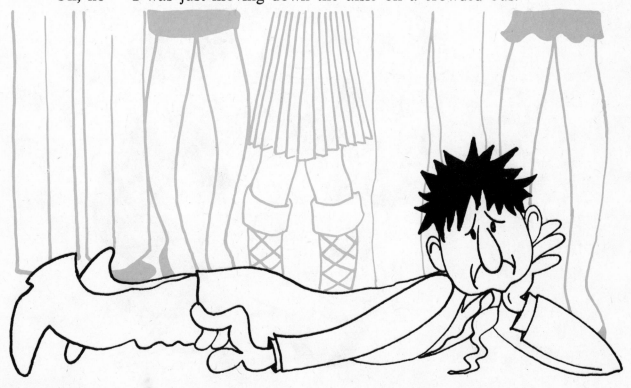

Librarian: Do you want something light or do you prefer the heavier books?
Reader: Oh, it doesn't matter — I have my car outside.

Lovely statue over there. Whose is it?
Oh, it belongs to the city.
No, no — I mean what is it of?
Granite, I guess.
But what does it represent?
About $50,000.
Thanks.

Father: Why were you kept after school today?
Son: I didn't know where the Azores were.
Father: Well, in the future, just remember where you put things.

Chemistry teacher: What can you tell me about nitrates?
Student: Well, I think they're cheaper than day rates.

Three somewhat hard-of-hearing ladies met on the street one day.
"Windy, isn't it?" said one.
"No, it's Thursday," said the second.
"So am I," said the third. "Let's all have a soda."

BONERS

Doctors who examine your eyes are called optimists.

An executive is a man who puts murderers to death.

An autobiography is a history of motor cars.

A psalmist is someone who tells fortunes by reading people's hands.

There are four symptoms of a cold. Two I forgot and the other two are too well-known to mention.

Milton was a blind poet who wrote "Paradise Lost." When his wife died, he wrote "Paradise Regained."

A fjord is a Swedish automobile.

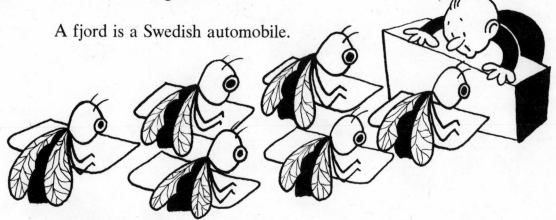

Mr. Koehler came to our schoolroom yesterday and lectured on destructive pests, a large number being present.

An Indian baby is called a caboose.

Lincoln wrote the Gettysburg Address while riding from Washington on an envelope.

The greatest miracle in the Bible was when Joshua told his son to stand still and he obeyed him.

The Golden Rule is: whoever finds gold first keeps it.

Davy Jones was an engineer killed in a train wreck.

A Scotland Yard is something less than three feet.

Gladiators are flowers grown from bulbs.

Poetic license is a license you get so that you can write poetry.

Romans are people who never stayed long in one place.

MARY'S LITTLE LAMB

Mary had a little car,
She drove in manner deft.
But every time she signaled right,
The little car turned left.

Mary had a little lamb,
Given her to keep.
It followed her around until
It died from lack of sleep.

Mary had a little lamb,
It drank some gasoline.
Then it wandered near a fire
And since has not benzine.

Mary had a little lamb,
A little pork, a little jam,
A little egg on toast,
A little potted roast,
A little stew with dumpling white,
A little shad,
An appetite.

Mary had a little lamb,
You've heard it oft before.
And then she passed her plate again
And had a little more.

Mary had a little lamb,
Its fleece was white as snow.
Mary passed the butcher shop,
But the lamb went by too slow.

Mary had a little watch,
She swallowed it — it's gone.
Now everywhere that Mary walks,
"Time marches on!"

Mary had a little lamb,
A lobster and some prunes,
A glass of milk, a piece of pie,
And then some macaroons;
It made the naughty waiters grin
To see her order so,
And when they carried Mary out,
Her face was white as snow.

Mary had a little lamb,
She put him on the shelf.
And every time he wagged his tail,
He spanked his little self.

TALL TALES

There's a girl in the country who has such bright red hair that when she leaves the house before sunrise, the roosters begin to crow.

Snowflakes fall so large in Oregon that parasol makers merely have to stick handles into them.

They are now building ferryboats so long that it takes two captains to command them, one at each end.

There is a pupil in a class who is so thin that when he stands sideways the teacher marks him absent.

There is a farm so big that when young couples go out to milk the cows their grandchildren bring back the milk.

One woman was such a meticulous housewife that she scrubbed the floors of her home until she fell through to the basement.

The fog is sometimes so thick in London that they use it to stuff pillows. By pouring ink on it and chopping it up, it may be sold for coal.

A man once grew so tall he had to climb a ladder to shave himself. And whenever he wanted to put his hands in his trouser pockets, he had to get down on his knees. He could eat nothing but freshly killed meat, else it would spoil before it reached his stomach. As it was, hot soup froze before it got there.

The ducks are so obliging on Long Island that when it comes time to roast them for dinner, they stuff themselves with sage and onions.

There's a fence in Indiana made of pine rails so crooked that every time a pig tries to crawl through it, it comes out on the same side from which it started.

There's one man we've heard tell about who has such a hard name, he spoils a dozen pens in signing one check.

He's so big that when the sun is out, people pay him to lie in his shade.

A photographer once took such a fine picture of a tree that it put forth leaves and bore fruit.

There's a lake in Minnesota that's so clear, you can look down into it and see them making tea in China.

A watchmaker has managed to make some of his watches go so fast they get 14 days in a week.

A thin man had to give up playing "Fetch the stick" with his dog. More often than not, the dog brought *him* back!

His eyes are so large that when he winks, the wind from his eyelids blows out a burning match.

One man devised an original way of fishing in winter. He would cut a hole in the ice that covered a lake, hold a watch over the hole, and when the fish came up to see what time it was, he'd hit them over the head with a club.

An artist once painted a picture of a cannon so realistically that when he finished it, it went off with a boom.

He has such a good temper that he hires himself out in summer to keep other people cool.

There are such tall trees in some parts of Wisconsin that it takes two men and a boy to look to the top of them. One looks until he gets tired, and another commences where he left off.

A barber is reported to have three razors, each sharper than the other. The first razor is so sharp that it cuts by itself. The second has to be held back. And the third cuts about a quarter of an inch before the edge.

One man has managed to live so quickly that he is now older than his father.

A man once found himself in the woods with a gun and only one bullet. He was walking alongside a river when he noticed ten ducks flying overhead in a straight line. He took sharp aim and fired the gun. The bullet passed through all ten ducks, killing them instantly. As the ducks fell, they broke a branch on a tree. The falling branch fell on a moose beneath the tree and killed it. As the moose died, it kicked a rabbit, which flew through the air and knocked the man into the river. He then waded out with his boots full of fish.

Five hundred soldiers attacked me, but I killed them all, one at a time.
How could you do that?
I surrounded them.

Sailor: Do you know that the Navy is building an aircraft carrier so large, the Pacific Ocean will have to be enlarged before it can turn around?
Airman: That's nothing. The Air Force is going to build a plane so large, we'll have to borrow air from Mars before we can fly it!

Two farmers' sons were talking.
"Say," said one, "my father once made such a good scarecrow, it frightened every crow off the farm for a whole summer."
"Yeah?" said the other. "My father once made one that scared the crows so much, they brought back the corn they'd swiped the year before!"

The drought sure has made the wheat short this year.
I'll say. I had to lather mine to mow it.

TALENTS

You seem to think I can't do a thing.
Not at all. You have more talent to the square head than anybody I know.

I'm studying to be a barber.
Will it take long?
No, I'm learning all the short cuts.

Client: I'll give you $100 to do my worrying for me.
Lawyer: Fine. Where's the hundred?
Client: That will be your first worry.

When you're an actor, you have to be able to turn your personality on
   and off like a faucet.
You must have a leaky washer — all I hear is a drip.

Did you notice how her voice filled the hall?
Yes, I noticed that a lot of people left to make room for it.

Visitor: What a glorious painting! I wish I could take those colors home!
Artist: You will — you're sitting on my palette.

My music is for the ages!
Yes — ages 5 to 10.

I have the leading part at the Town Theater.
Star of the show?
No, head usher.

I was a struggling writer once.
Did you sell anything?
Yes — my watch and my overcoat.

Plumber: I'm sorry I'm late, but I just couldn't get here any sooner.
Householder: Well, time hasn't been wasted. While we were waiting for you, I taught my wife how to swim.

Lawyer: As your attorney, I'm sorry I couldn't do any more for you.
Prisoner: Thanks. Ten years was plenty.

Visitor: What does that painting represent?
Artist: That is a cow grazing.
Visitor: Where is the grass?
Artist: The cow has eaten it.
Visitor: But where is the cow?
Artist: You don't suppose she'd be fool enough to stay there after she'd eaten all the grass, do you?

Oh, I'm a good speaker. Why, I once spoke to thousands of people at Madison Square Garden.
What did you say?
"Peanuts, popcorn, cigarettes, candy . . ."

Diner: Do you ever play anything by request?

Musician: Certainly, sir.

Diner: Then I wonder if you'd play dominoes until I've finished my lunch.

Bald-headed man: It isn't fair — charging me full price for cutting my hair!

Barber: Sir, we charge you only half price for cutting it — and half for *looking* for it!

Fussy Customer: I want a haircut. Don't cut off any on the top or the side or in the middle. Do you know what I want?

Barber: Yes — a noise with the scissors.

Do you understand why Robin Hood robbed only the rich?

Sure — because the poor had no money.

Woman: $80 for that hat? Why, there isn't anything on it!

Milliner: Madam, you are paying for the restraint.

MATTER OF OPINION

Marge: Gosh, Mabel, what have you done to your hair? It looks like a wig!
Mabel: It *is* a wig!
Marge: Goodness, you'd never know it!

How did you enjoy the movie?
It was simply awful. I could hardly sit through it a second time.

What did you think of the new play that opened last night?
Very refreshing — I felt like a new man when I woke up.

Tourist: Is it true that an alligator won't harm you if you carry a torch?
Guide: It depends on how fast you carry it, I reckon.

Never put off till tomorrow what you can put off for good.

What must a girl do to have soft hands?
Nothing!

Mary: Peanuts are fattening.
Cary: How do you know?
Mary: Did you ever see a skinny elephant?

TRAVEL

Traveler: I'm in a great hurry to get to Los Angeles. How soon can you get me there?

Ticket Agent: The train will leave in a few minutes and will get you there in 20 hours. Tomorrow evening, though, we're putting on a new train that will get you there in 17 hours.

Traveler: All right, I'll wait until tomorrow evening.

Guide: Here, ladies and gentlemen, is a magnificent waterfall. May I ask the ladies to cease talking for a moment so that we may hear the roar of the waters?

One-way ticket to Toronto, please.
Do you wish to go by Buffalo?
Certainly not — by train.

Can I catch the three o'clock train to Burlington?
That depends on how fast you can run. It left here ten minutes ago.

"I'm sorry, ma'am," said the conductor, "but your ticket is for Chicago, and this train is going to Washington, D.C."

"My goodness!" exclaimed the lady. "Does the engineer know he's going in the wrong direction?"

Has he traveled much?
Oh, yes — he's been to at least half the places on his suitcase labels.

Can you tell me how to get to Riversburg from here?
Well, go back a couple of miles and take the first road to the left. No, maybe it's the second road to the left. Come to think of it, stranger, if I were trying to get to Riversburg, I wouldn't start from here at all.

Mountain Guide: Be very careful now, folks — this is the most dangerous place of all. But if you do fall, on your way down remember to look to your right. You'll never again in your life see a view like that.

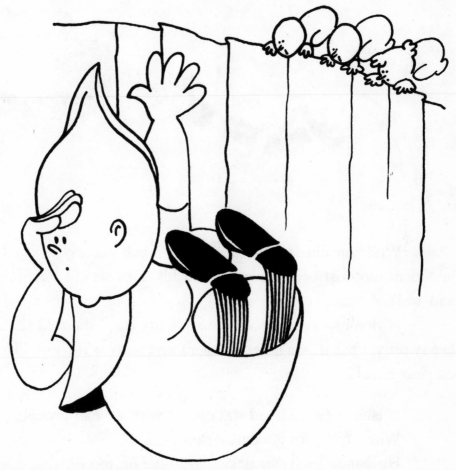

Jack: Where did you go on your trip?

Mack: Well, we were going to take a trip around the world, but we changed our mind and went somewhere else instead.

A foreign visitor was viewing the spectacle of Niagara Falls. "Millions of gallons of water drop down every minute," said a guide impressively.

"Really?" said the visitor, who did not seem to be especially awed. "And how many in a day?"

"Oh, billions — just billions," replied the guide.

"Hmm-m," mused the visitor. "Runs all night, too, I suppose?"

Why are you leaving Philadelphia to go and live in Cleveland?

To be nearer my daughter who lives in Seattle.

While an old lady tried without much success to get her car started, an impatient motorist behind her honked his horn steadily. At last, the lady got out and walked back.

"I don't seem to be able to start my car," she told the driver of the other car sweetly, "but if you'll get up there and start it for me, I'll stay here and lean on your horn!"

Husband (at railroad station): I wish we had brought the TV set with us.
Wife: Why, for goodness' sake?
Husband: I left our tickets at home on top of it.

Give me a round-trip ticket, please.
Where to?
Back here.

Woman: Can I get a ticket for Brattleboro?
Ticket Agent: Where is Brattleboro?
Woman: Right over there — he's my little boy.

Did you stop off in Egypt on your trip around the world?
Oh, yes.
Did you go up the Nile?
Yes — *marvelous* view from the top!

Ha, ha, ha! I sure put one over on the railroad today.

How?

I bought a round-trip ticket to San Francisco and I'm never coming back.

How are we on gas?

Well, the indicator says half, but I don't know if it means half full or half empty.

Why are you driving so fast?

Because there aren't any brakes on the car and I want to get home before I have an accident.

How are your driving lessons coming along?

Good. The road is beginning to turn when I do.

I got rid of that noise in the rear of my car.

How did you do it?

I made her sit up front with me.

This train goes to Buffalo and points west.

Well, I want a train that gets to Syracuse and I don't care which way it points.

Passenger: Conductor, does this train stop at San Francisco?

Conductor: Well, if it doesn't, there'll be a big splash!

Taxi Driver: I can't stop the car! I've lost control!
Passenger: For Heaven's sake, turn off the meter!

Freddy: Did you ride any of those jinrikishas while you were in the Orient?
Teddy: Yes — and they have horses that look just like men!

I suppose you've seen the whole world?
Oh, yes — what there is of it.

Passenger: What's the use of your timetable? The trains never keep time.
Conductor: Well, how would you know they were late if it wasn't for
  the timetable?

So you're not going to Bermuda this year?
No, it's Miami we're not going to this year. It was Bermuda we didn't go
  to last year.

Your car is at the door.
Yes, I can hear it knocking.

I once ran into a flock of geese while driving 70 miles an hour.
Gosh, I'll bet you were scared.
I was covered with gooseflesh.

Why are you stopping the car?
Well, my directions say to turn south and follow the bus. We'll have to
  wait until one comes along.

I see Harry is now riding around in a bigger car.
He's getting up in the world, eh?
No, his old car was wrecked and so he's riding in a bus.

What are we doing on the road to Kansas City when we're supposed to
  be going to Philadelphia?
Oh, it's a better road.

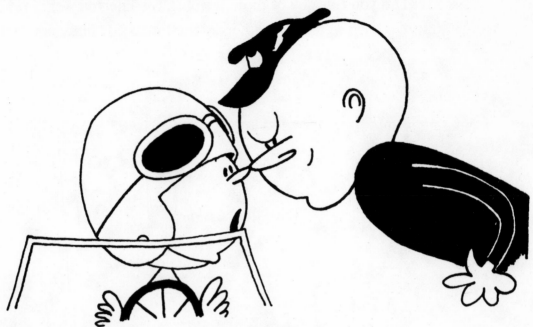

Policeman: You're under arrest for speeding.

Motorist: I wasn't speeding, officer — but I passed a couple of fellows
who were.

Say, the starter button is missing from your car.
Yes, I know — I just got the car back from the auto laundry.

Nervous Passenger: Please don't drive so fast around the corners. It
frightens me.

Taxi Driver: Just do what I do, lady — shut your eyes when we come to
a corner.

Small-car Motorist: Put a glass of water in the radiator, a thimbleful of
oil in the crankcase, and a demitasse of gas in the tank. I think that will be all.

Service Station Attendant: Couldn't I sneeze in your tires?

How did you like the Swiss Alps?
Nicest people I ever met!

How far is it to the next town?
Oh, about five miles. You can walk it easily in an hour, if you run.